Love
Through My Eyes

Inspired Poems

Shantell N. Parson

Love Through My Eyes

Copyright © 2021 by *Shantell N. Parson*

All rights reserved. No part of this publication may be reproduced, distributed, or transmitted in any form or by any means, including photocopying, recording, or other electronic or mechanical methods, without the prior written permission of the author, except in the case of brief quotations embodied in critical reviews and certain other non-commercial uses permitted by copyright law.

ISBN
978-1-954932-36-4 (Paperback)
978-1-954932-35-7 (eBook)

No one is perfect. We give, we take. We win, we lose. It is never about how you overcame your challenges but; the fact that you overcame them and moved forward.

This book is dedicated to the loves I have had, lost, and the ones that have loved me enough to stay.

I love you;

To the future and beyond!

Table of Contents

I am His Beloved

I am a Man

A Brother's Love

You Are

Proud

First Kiss

I Use to Love You

One Day

Lies

I Almost Gave Up on You

Love Is . . .

Excuse Me

Over It!

Strong

Til the Time Comes

I Need A Man

I Need a Woman

I Am in Love

Marry Me

I Do

Beautiful

Trust In You?

Power of Love

I Submit to You

Falling In Love

Seeing You

In Your Arms

Lips

All Night Long

Love Through My Eyes

I Am His Beloved...

*Through my highs
and my lows.
I am His beloved.
His grace and mercy cling to me.
I am His beloved.
A deeper love
I have with Him.
From the beginning to the end,
I am His beloved.
He loved me
Before I could even breathe.
Knowing the paths
I would choose to take
No matter the wrongs
and all my mistakes.
I am His beloved.
He delights in me,
Don't you see?
He lives in me.
I am His beloved.*

Shantell Parson

His love is everlasting,

Full of peace and hope.

He delights in me.

When I have no words;

my throat is dry,

and the tears are flowing from my eyes.

Bills are due,

I have no money

not knowing which way to turn

or what to do.

All I have is my Faith in You.

The love in my heart,

and a worn-out bible

from many years of use.

There,

In the distance

A whisper of words.

"You are my beloved. Rest assure I know your needs and will provide. Grace and mercy is upon you. You are my beloved and I delight in you."

It doesn't matter where you come from or where you are going. Someone once told me, "Shantell, Life is all around you." And I couldn't agree more. I always say life is like a roller coaster; it has its highs and lows; and its ups and downs. Life is a whirl wind of emotions. You scream, you cry, you laugh, you get scared but it is the anticipation that captures you the most.

We all love different people in so many different ways.

Sit back and ride my ride of; Love Through My Eyes. Before you begin to read take a minute and think about all the loves you have had and lost. Now think about the ones that stayed. With the joy you feel in your heart I pray that at least one poem touches you with that same amount of joy.

Let's begin . . .

I am a Man

I am a man.

That's how my mom raised me.

Never to raise my hand

Or fist to any woman!

But,

to love and support her wants and needs.

I am still growing

and developing me.

So, I can be the proper man

I am being taught to be.

Right now,

I am fixing me.

Going to school, learning to cook,

and how to balancing my checkbook!

I am going to be a blessing,

to the woman God puts in my life.

So, don't think me rude

if I bypass you.

Cuz, I don't have time for games

or people out to use me.

Love Through My Eyes

You see materialistic things

mean nothing to me.

I am a man

with goals and dreams.

My mother didn't raise me

to be nobody's fool.

My woman has got to have faith, class

and respect for herself.

Not posting what she has all over social media!

I am going to need a strong woman

standing next to me.

Nothing less will do

for the man I inspire to be.

I am a man.

Thanks to my mom who raised me!

A Brother's Love
Dedicated to my brother, Eric.

When I was picked on

because of my size.

You defended me,

and was ready to fight.

When I cried

from the hard life we lived.

You promised me,

Everything would be alright.

When I got pregnant at 16 years of age.
You yelled and scolded me

And said,

"No worries Shan, I love you anyway."

In those days you were always there.

Laughing, loving, and caring too.

Even though we worked each other's nerves,

Cuz that's what brothers and sisters often do.

As we got older,

You changed and pulled away.

But in my heart, I ALWAYS carry you.

I carry the memories of you and me.

Love Through My Eyes

Hand in hand against the toughest enemy.

You are my brother,

Forever and always!

I loved you then

And love you still.

Nothing will change that in my heart.

No man will ever be able to play that part.

Know that I love you.

And always will.

Thank you for keeping me safe and sound.

You did your job well

Despite our paths in life.

Thank you for your love;

A brother's love,

I pray will always be around.

You Are

Dedicated to my best friend, Tasha.

You are;

My sister in Christ

and my best friend.

My ride or die chick;

Friends 'til the end.

We laugh,

We cry,

We understand each other's nods.

We agree to disagree

when we don't see eye to eye.

I love you,

and you love me.

No man can change

the relationship we share.

You are;

in my heart

and a part of me.

Like Sister Sledge,

"We Are Family!"

Love Through My Eyes

No matter the miles

that are between us.

I got your back

and you got mine.

The talks, the shots, and the fun we have.

You are;

More than family

more than a friend.

You are truly;

My Best Friend,

My partner in crime

My sister forever,

'Til the end of time.

Best friends forever!!

Proud

So,

you think because I am hard on you

that I love you less.

My dear child

how wrong you are.

I never say hurtful words

that put you down.

But I am honest and true,

Like I want you to be too.

Sure, I say,

"That was a dumb thing to do!"

Because it was!

Never have I called you dumb

Or out of name.

You have no idea

The unconditional love I have for you.

All I am trying to do

is guide you to be

A stronger better You!!!

You listen to the people in the streets.

Love Through My Eyes

Instead of the parent

that has been around all of your life!

Now how crazy does that sound?

All I want is the best for you.

To see you succeed way past me.

People are looking to see you fail.

They will walk away as you rot in jail.

Never let the enemy see you sweat.

Are the words my mother taught me.

Thanks mom!!

Cuz 'til this day

These words ain't never lie!!

I am not your enemy!

However, I am

Your protector

Your lender

Your guide

Your provider

Your parent

And

As you get older

Your friend.

I am even the person

Shantell Parson

That washes your dirty underwear!

From the beginning I carried you having nothing but unconditional love

Pouring out of my heart.

And here you are acting

Like I owe you!

Listen to me,

And hear me good!

I owe you nothing.

As your mother your parent

I am doing my job!

The world isn't roses.

It's thistles and thorns

Nor is it sugar drops and lollipops

As the game goes.

So why do you think

I would sugar coat life and truth for you

Learn your lessons

And learn them well.

Hear the words I say to you

Because you only have 1 at the end of the day.

1

Life to live with no do overs.

1

Love Through My Eyes

Ride to ride before game over.

1

Unconditional love of another.

1

Woman who birthed you

Which is your mother.

So, take the time to stop and think,

when someone wants to take you down the wrong path.

Turn to them and tell them

NO!!!

This is not how I was taught!

This is not the path for me!

This is not my destiny!

I am wonderfully and talentedly made!

I am going to be the man

My mother raised!

And when you are ready,

Here I will be.

Waiting with open arms

Proud as can be!

The Beginning

In the beginning we think
we are so in love.
The age varies when we experience
our
1st crush,
1st kiss,
1st love,
and the pain of our 1st heart break.
There are never any words to
prepare us for life during
and after love regardless of age.
I will always remember my 1st love.
This section is
about when toys are a thing of the past
and love takes its place.

First Kiss

When I met you, my heart stood still.

I couldn't wait to bump into you

or see your smile.

Finally getting the courage to talk to you.

And you didn't turn me down.

Looking forward to the time we spend.

Needing it to go slow.

Being young and inexperienced

not knowing what to do.

Seen it done a million times;

But never had it done to me.

Nervous as hell hands shaking.

So many thoughts in my mind.

Wondering if you are as nervous as I am?

Screw it!

As I throw caution to the wind.

Here I go!

I lean into you

You lean into me.

Our lips connect

Shantell Parson

And there is it

My first kiss!

Practice makes perfect

We do it again!

Relaxing into your arms

I exhale the breath I didn't know I was holding.

I never knew kissing was this exciting.

Feeling the connection between you and me.

Something is growing

and changing my body.

I want to do more

I want to go further,

But can we take our time and just go slow?

You were my first kiss

My first crush

I will remember you forever.

I Use to Love You

When we 1st met

we instantly click.

Friends to the end

or so I thought.

There was no Prince Charming or Cinderella here.

More like Bonnie and Clyde

with a twist of hood life.

Sarcasm and wit spared at no expense.

I could be me and you were free to be you.

There wasn't anything we couldn't talk about

Chillin' on the stoop.

And then it happened,

I became depend on you.

Your honesty and laughter

Was contagious to me.

The time we spent together

Was second nature to me.

Enlightening my heart and soul.

I had come to the realization

that I loved you.

And it didn't take me long

Shantell Parson

to realize that you loved me too.

But you being a control freak

wouldn't allow yourself to admit

your feelings of affection you carry for me.

Heart broken and ashamed,

I cried myself to sleep

mortified for being a fool.

Telling myself it was just infatuation and to move on.

So, every now and then,

I reach out to you.

Allowing you to stay in control and me be the fool.

But the hard truth of the matter is

you will never be in love with me.

It breaks my heart

when I think about us;

and all the things that we COULD be.

I know now that you did love me.

I miss the friendship we forged together

Ill never forget you

And those sweet lips.

Nor will I forget

How,

I use to love you.

One Day

One day

I will get to show you my love.

One day

You will feel what it is like to have all of me.

One day

You will show me your love for me.

One day

You will whisper sweet words in my ear.

One day.

Just one day is what I crave.

At times it seems to be so much to ask for.

One day.

One day in time is all I seek.

24 hours

1440 minutes

86400 seconds.

One day.

To be so close yet so far away.

To not have the feel of your touch.

One day.

A day in time for a lover's kiss.

Shantell Parson

A day of romance and erotic bliss.

One day.

So, until the day that you are hear with me.

Sending you love my love.

Until. . .

One day.

Lies...

It's funny how lying

comes so easily to you.

It seems to come 1st nature

like a second layer of skin on you.

365

And on leap years too.

Yet here you stand;

saying you want all of me.

Please tell me you're joking?

You gotta be kidding me?

It took me some time

to finally see the real, you.

And now that I do,

I am better off without you!

Don't get me wrong,

I wish you the best.

But, the best of me

You will never see or get!!

The time has come to say Goodbye.

I've packed your shit

Shantell Parson

Tired of your lies.

No longer will I be the fool

at your side

Watch my hips sway from side to side

For the very last time.

Keep the key

I've changed the locks

and changed my number too.

Closing the chapter of you in my life

It's Over…

You're dismissed

With all of your lies!!

I Almost Gave Up On You

I almost gave up on you.

I didn't think you were real.

I had these dreams of you in my mind.

Praying and hoping,

Day and night.

But as time went by it seemed like just a dream.

I mean who was gonna love the battered me?

My heart broken and in pieces laid out on the floor.

Bleeding from scars of casual war.

I had locked what was left of my broken heart.

Far away from every touch.

I almost gave up on you.

You see I spent so many nights,

Crying and wishing that I was dead.

Cuz that was the only way to stop the pain.

To stop the hurt.

To no longer feel anything of this world.

Hard to believe even now that you are real.

'Til one day you appeared.

Picking up the pieces of my heart

Shantell Parson

Promising me that this won't end.

Telling me things like,

"I am your peace."

And your future is here with me.

I'm tired of fighting past my tears.

Not wanting to put my past on you.

Finding myself questioning everything you do.

Yet, still you have patience with me.

Just when I thought I was happy being alone.

You showed up with words of love.

Words like…

"I am in love with you"

"Trust in me I won't hurt you"

Everyday you prove your love for me.

I can't believe how I almost walked away,

I almost gave up on you.

Love is...

Love is

patient,

Love is

kind.

Love is

always having that person on your mind.

In your heart you carry them.

Deep inside is where they'll always be.

Their laughter stirs something in you;

Their words of kindness carries you.

Through the storms you face in your life.

Through the long days,

And hot summer nights.

They make you smile every day.

You feel their love from miles away.

Never forget them when life gets tough.

Because they'll be the one's that will be strong for you.

So when you are sad and feeling blue,

Remember that someone special loves you.

And your happiness means the world to them.

They will lift your spirits,

Shantell Parson

So, please don't cry.

But if you have to shed a tear,

They will be there in a heartbeat.

To listen, to hold, and be a friend,

weathering the storms through thick and thin.

Thank you for being that friend to me.

I love you

And you love me,

Don't ever be afraid to lean on me.

My love is here

In every way.

Excuse Me

Is it my beauty

Or my booty that you see?

Can you look me in eyes?

Or will you always look toward my breast and thighs?

All I want is to be noticed for the woman in me.

I am more than these succulent hips that go deep.

When you look at me,

is bustin a nut the only thing you see?

I'm not about the booty calls

And secret rendezvous.

Tired of the games

That boys to men play

Thinking that mess is cute.

Now, don't get me wrong some women play too.

And then got the nerve to say

Where the good women and men at?

You'll played us too many times

And made us look like fools.

I am a passionate woman.

I love to be touched.

Shantell Parson

I enjoy laughing
And flirtatious innuendos.
But at the end of the day
I enjoy my man next to me.
If you gonna step
To a woman like me
You can't say,
"Excuse me Ms., what that mouth do?"
You can't step to me trying to keep face
with partners in crime.
I'm a lady with a lot of class.
But, don't get this Jersey girl twisted
I will blast dat ass.
I'm a good woman
Who won't settle for less.
You will be dismissed and blocked
For foolishness.
So, when you get the nerve
And say,
"Excuse me Ms."
Be ready to answer,
What do you really want from me?
My time is too precious to waste
On someone who can't
emotionally and mentally
Stimulate me.

Over It!

Tired of your lies,
And your played out games.
You think you got the better of me.
Hmm. Think again.
I'm So Over It!
Wanna be friends
out to use me.
But, when I call on you,
Your gone like the wind.
Delete!
I'm So Over It!!
To those of you
who hang around.
Who look and smile in my face.
But when I turn my back
got something smart to say.
Hmmm.
Delete!
I'm So Over It!!
Working a job

Shantell Parson

Unappreciated.

Underpaid.

People always yelling.

The days are long.

The hours go by slow.

My head half down

And some days

all I want to do is cry.

This will not be the death of me!!

I'm So Over It!!

Over It!
Continued...

Pushing everyday

with all that I have.

Finding the joys

to keep me grounded in life.

Hear me when I say,

My joy you can't have!

My laughter will never end!

My smile will be bright!

I will be Alright.

I will be me.

Strong like I am.

You will not be the death of me!

Hmmm

I'm So Over It!!

Right now, there is someone who feels hopeless and unloved. Someone in need of a friend, a kind word, a hug, a home, or even just to feel safe. The list can go on and on. Be a kind word to someone and never forget that you don't know the path they walk. It could be the last time you talk to them and you may never know it. Never be too busy to tell someone that you love them while you have the time.

To the men, women, and children. You are not alone! There is someone that cares and would be sadden by the loss of your life.

Be STRONG!

Strong

STOP!
PLEASE!
WAIT!
May I talk to you?
Before you do something
You can't take back.
Let me tell you;
You are BEAUTIFUL!
I know things seem hard
and you think no one sees you.

But know that I am here
and I see you very clear.
I see the tears you cry and
the voice that screams from the inside.
the cruel things people say and do.
I see the hurt and despair
they cause you.
Trust me

I've been there too.
Not knowing which way to turn
or what to do.
People seeking to destroy the beauty in you.
With their harsh words
cutting deeper than any knife could!
Powerful fist
That drives the very breathe outta out you!
But let me tell you;
this is not your time!
Your life is a precious gift
part of the immaculate design!

Shantell Parson

One thing I have learned in my years on this earth.
People will talk.
Good or bad.
Right or wrong.
It doesn't matter
as their goal is to hurt.

Thinking because they know of you

That they can talk about or judge

the nature of you.
But the only person that knows YOU is YOU!!!

Hear me when I say

No one can Make or Break You!!
If you don't allow them too.
Don't allow them to win.
Why give them that power over you?

Hear me when I say
You ARE BEAUTIFUL!
Do you hear what I am telling you?
I will NEVER lie or abuse you.
Anytime of the day or night,
You find you are in need of a friend.
I'll be here to inspire you

Lift you up and pray for and with you
Now is not the time to end
This awesome gift of life.
You are
STRONG
TALENTED
AND BEAUTIFUL
Perfect the way God made you!
You are my friend

Love Through My Eyes

So please don't think you are alone
DON'T LET HATE TAKE YOU AWAY FROM ME!!
DON'T BELIEVE YOU MEAN NOTHING
When you are EVERYTHING!!!

Never forget how

Strong you really are.

'Til the Time Comes

Here we are.

Me and you.

You and me.

Your arms wrapped around me,

And mines around you.

Vibin' and chillin'

Just us 2.

The movie playing

As you caress my back.

I look up at you

And you down at me.

My mind screaming,

ASK HIM!

ASK HIM!

ASK HIM!

AND SEE!

I open my mouth about to ask.

What do you see when you look at me?

Do you only see me as a friend?

Do you only see the beauty of the skin?

Love Through My Eyes

Or maybe,

Just maybe you see deeper than that?

Yes,

We are friends and I have grown to care for you.

Loving our conversations

and the things we do.

You know foreplay is nothing,

Between me and you.

Cuz,

Talking ish to each is what we do.

We have had our share of drama

mistakes we've made in the past.

Not trying to rock the boat,

Just keep it study and on course.

But, in the time

that we have spent together,

I see what you don't see in you.

Never will I sleep on you.

You're smart, funny, and thuggish too.

Your charm and your wit;

keep me close to you.

Truth be told

One day I want you to be mine.

Shantell Parson

Nothing but the truth,

is what I expect from you.

However, my heart not willing

to take the blow.

The disappointment of you just seeing

the outside physical beauty of me.

So, I lower my gaze,

and let things be.

Smiling and closing my mouth.

I steal a kiss.

Waiting is what I will do.

Til the time comes

That you see the woman and love

wanting and waiting for you.

I Need A Man

I need a man,

To see the beauty in me.

The kinda of beauty that goes beyond simple vision.

A man that can see my complexity.

Finding it charming,

cuz he just really gets me.

I need a man,

that will support me.

No, I don't particularly mean or need your money,

But;

your hand to hold when I am scared.

I need a man,

that is strong when I am weak.

A man who will protect and defend me.

I need a man,

whose love surrounds me like armory.

Gentle hands caressing me,

kisses passionate.

He knows I am his

And

Shantell Parson

He is mine.

Yes,

I need a man,

Who puts family 1st.

Cuz that is where his heart lives most.

I need a man,

who talks in words of

WE and US.

Cuz he values the gift of love we share.

I need a man,

I can call mine.

Day in and day out.

As we build our empire together.

Trusting when we say,

"Babe, I got you!"

We got each other's back.

Cuz,

That's how we do.

No man or woman can tear or break us!

Yes!

Yes!

I need a man,

In my life

Love Through My Eyes

That won't hurt or use me to fit his needs.

But, respects and cherishes the woman he has in me.

Thanking the men of my past,

Cuz now he got the best they never had.

He got the woman of his dreams.

He got this woman…

Talented,

Gifted

Beautiful

ME!!

I Need A Woman

I need a woman

Who is down for only me.

Willing to stand strong at my side

and not sneak around behind my back.

I need a woman

Who has an intimate relationship with God.

A woman who will pray for me and us.

Keeping family up lifted and first.

I need a woman

That leaves the tricks for kids.

That isn't about the drama or the b.s.

I don't need nor what that in my life.

I need a woman

That knows how to dress

A woman with style class and finesse.

She gotta know that her body is mine

And mine is hers.

So that means we only share behind closed doors.

You see

I'm a private person and my woman must respect that.

Love Through My Eyes

I'm not judging her by her size

She gotta know it's her mind

I am truly attracted to most.

I need a woman

Who knows how to cook.

I don't mean the stuff in a can or a frozen meal.

She gotta know how to cook

Like momma and big momma use too.

I need a woman

That will love me for me.

She needs to silly and laugh.

A woman that can be strong when I am weak.

Willing to hold us down

when I am unable to lead.

I need a woman

That is satisfied with who she sees.

Not out to use, manipulate or steal from me.

She accepts my flaws

and the man in me.

I need a woman

Like you need a man.

I want to be happy too

while I still can.

Shantell Parson

Why should I settle for anything less?

I need a woman

Not out to judge me by my past

Because it is behind me.

I need a woman

I can bring home to mom

A woman that can hold her own and is strong.

I know there is a woman

waiting for me.

A woman that is only mine

who's love belongs to only me.

Marriage is not something that you should enter into lightly. Being with someone in good and bad times. Sometimes it works out and sometimes it doesn't. I am not an expert on love by any means.

There comes a time in our lives when we get imitation love and don't realize it until it is too late.

As we go through the highs and lows and want to give up someone comes along and we realize just what we have been missing…

I am in Love

I am in Love

with a wonderful man.

I am in Love.

every time he touches my hand.

I never knew of a love this powerful

I never knew of a love this incredible.

I am in Love.

I will proclaim it from here to there.

In the sky

on the ground;

in and out of every state and town.

I am in Love.

This man is intelligent and true to his heart.

Every word he speaks

embraces every inch of me.

I plan to love this man with all my might.

You are in my heart

and on my mind.

You are a man of pure gold.

Strong,

Love Through My Eyes
Priceless, and
Simply Irresistible.
You are just beautiful.
I am in Love.

Marry Me

I have nothing to offer you but my love.

Won't you please,

Marry me?

I am far from perfect

but my love for you is.

Will you please,

Marry me?

We will disagree

and I may even make you cry.

But,

when we make up new sparks will fly.

Don't let our love pass you by.

Just say yes

and

Marry me.

I'll cook you breakfast in bed.

Pull you into my arms

and we will slow dance.

All you have to do is

Marry me.

Love Through My Eyes
You complete me
when you stand by my side.
There is no one else on this earth
that can love you the way I can.
Make me happy
make me proud.
As you stand by my side
for the rest of our life's.
Just say yes
Marry Me.

I Do

On this day we say

I Do.

Here I vow to love you.

You have my heart, my love, my life.

I promise to carry you through

the distance of time and space.

This love we share has changed my life.

To put it simply

you complete me.

I knew in my soul

That I was going to make you mine.

The good the bad

the ups and the downs

will never shake this commitment

we are taking here and now.

God bless this union.

I pray to thee.

I've waited so long for this day to come true.

As I stand here and declare my love to you.

Sharing my love with you through eternity.

Love Through My Eyes

Know this ring means so much to me.

It represents a solid commitment of trust & honesty.

Here you stand freely

bestowing unto me.

From the start you had my heart.

Today, tomorrow, forever

I promise to be only yours!

Beautiful

When you look at me
with the passion and love;
you carry for me.
You are
beautiful to me.
The smile on your face
when you're laughing
and playing with me.
You are
beautiful to me.
Dressed in jeans and a tee;
those big arms and hands
waiting to embrace me.
Looking sexy and catching my eye.
You are
beautiful to me.
Loving how we talk and tease.
You've had my heart,
from the start.
You are

Love Through My Eyes
beautiful to me.
When you walk up behind me
and seductively kiss my neck.
Making my heart skip a beat.
My heart, my love, and my support
will always be yours.
You are
beautiful to me.

Trust in You?

You have the nerve to ask me to trust and believe in you!

But you haven't been forthcoming,

In telling me the truth.

You stopped talking and communicating with me.

Down grating me to less than what I am.

I opened my eyes and started to see,

That you were never strong

but weak.

Because there you are clear as day,

In her arms

and holding her hand.

My entire future laid to rest!

Please tell me how you would feel?

I want to know would you love me still?

After the time we have been together.

Would you give me your trust if I asked it of you?

Would you hold the line and wait for me to come to you?

Would your heart break at the thought of the marriage we have?

To see me with another man!

Would it bother you at all?

Love Through My Eyes

Would you feel the lump of doubt and disgust stuck hard in your chest?

Wonder if everything I said was a lie?

I mean after all I won't return or answer your calls!!

Would you fight or walk away?

When all I can say is, "Trust me please."

Is that enough to calm your nerves?

Or would the man who loved me go completely berserk?!!

I am trying my best not to call you out your name.

Because my heart is broken in a thousand ways.

The tears won't stop running from my eyes.

I screamed until I was hoarse inside.

And all I wanted to do was die.

My body numb

As thoughts about you with her

and her with you!!

TRUST!!!

TRUST!!!

TRUST!!!

You say.

Trust in what?

You broke your vows.

How am I supposed to believe what you say?

Tell me please,

Shantell Parson

Why should I stay?

You left me alone in the dark.

Could you?

Would you?

Trust me at this point?

You did something you said you would never do.

You broke our wedding vows!!!

You Fool!!!

But now,

I have a question for you.

Will you fight for me as I did for you?

Power of Love

Never will you be alone again.
Sitting in the dark
questioning the things of the past.
In the dark I'll hold your hand;
feeding you my strength
and all that I am.
The nights you toss and turn
and can not sleep.
I will be there,
just turn around and lean on me.
Never will you wonder
where my heart is;
when you turn around,
I will always be right here.
Cheering you on in all you do.
Supporting your decisions and trusting in you.
To the end of time I am committed to you.
Tell me what I can do to build our future nest;
I made a decision to love and honor you,
I made my decision to be completely devoted to you.

Shantell Parson

So please do not hide yourself from me,
there will never be a taboo topic in privacy.
The dark is no place for you to be.
Look into my eyes and grab my hand.
I won't let go babe, I understand;
the battle you fight within everyday.
No longer will you fight or struggle alone.
I am more than willing to be your shield,
pick me up and use me at will.
This is why fate drew you to me.
This is God's divine plan, don't you see?
For you to be a whole and completed man;
you need the love of one woman.
I am an extended part of you.
Don't you feel it in your heart too?
You know what I speak to be true.
It's in my smile and laughter
when I am with you.
It's the way I carry myself,
as I stand taller next to you.
No longer will you hear the noises
or the things that go bump in the night.
Because I am here to be your Light.

I Submit to You

I submit all of me.

My love,

My pain,

My darkest fears.

Who I am;

I'm in your care.

My pleasures,

My fantasies,

My lustful desires.

Are yours to carry and fulfill.

I submit to you.

Allow me to carry the load

Of you and me.

In my gift of submission

I am strong enough for you.

Here I sit on bended knees.

Obeying.

Surrendering.

I submit to you.

My support you will always have.

Pushing you to succeed,

Shantell Parson

Being quiet,

When my flesh wants to speak.

Praying for both you and me.

I submit to you.

You are my lifetime.

Respect and trust

In the woman in me.

I am everything that you need.

Never will I tear you down

Or think you weak.

You are the head

I follow you.

Stake your claim upon me.

Be my protector

and fill my needs.

Take care of and treasure me.

Show me I am wanted;

And I will show you

how much you are needed.

I submit to you.

The Next Level

Behind closed doors we make love. The physical love between two people is a beautiful thing. The bliss of touching each other's body and releasing the day on a whole new level.

Fallen In Love

In your eyes I see the sun rise
and I know that is where I want to be.
The love of one man
holding my hand,
Umm
that is heaven to me.
Your mouth speaks pure love
From sunrise to sunset
every time our eyes meet.
Your tongue is blade sharp
but at the same time
gentle
when you feast upon me.
I love the feel of your hands
as they glide across
my curvaceous body.
What I feel is more than just
the bliss of our bodies.
As we love
one on one

Love Through My Eyes

like it should be.

Your style, your charm, your personality

and your intelligence is becoming to me.

There is no pretending

I am

who I am

when you place your loving arms around me.

Loving my smile, my style, my strength

and the woman I have come to be.

You see me for me

and look past the sexy exterior on me.

I need to let you know right here and right now

that I have completely fallen in love with you.

Seeing You

I look forward to seeing you.

To feel your lips

kissing me.

The way you grab and caress me.

Your smile,

Sexy.

Your walk,

Straight hood.

Conversation,

On point.

And a shit talker too.

I bit my lip

thinking

of the things you do to me.

Kisses,

Passionate.

Hands,

Firm.

Touches,

Gentle as you stroke my body.

Love Through My Eyes

Your mouth on my breast.

Sucking and teasing.

your tongue flicking

Over and over and over again.

My nipples hard

from the pleasures you're giving me.

Those chocolate eyes

look down at me,

right before you flip me

And

cover my body.

Your erection

Wanting.

Needing.

Craving me.

The warmth and cream

between my thick thighs.

My hands on your head

as you part my legs

and feast on my body.

I moan your name

in a soft plea.

Wanting you to stop

Shantell Parson

and plunge deep inside of me.

Your mouth covering mine;

Lovin' the way I taste on those beautiful soft lips.

Your hard shaft

driving in and out of me.

My orgasm running

all over you.

My legs shaking

From the things you do.

Mmmmmmm

Baby,

cum for me.

Give me all of you.

And when we're done

you hold me,

and I hold you.

How I look forward

to seeing you.

In Your Arms

In your arms,
is where I want to be.
On cold winter nights
snuggled next to you.
When the world seems heavy
and coming down on me,
In your arms,
is where I want to be.
Locked in an embrace
of your love for me.
Spending nights in our bed for 2,
Laughing and talking like we do.
And those moments
when I get you in the mood,
turning up the heat to your heart and soul.
Becoming all you desire and more.
In your arms is where I want to be.
After making love between the sheets,
As we drift off into a blissful sleep.
Loving the way you snuggle up behind me.
In your arms,

Shantell Parson

is where I wanna be.

Sharing our love for eternity.

At the end of the day

30 years from now,

As grey and silver hair replace the black.

And grandkids have climbed up and down our laps.

Hand in hand,

Heart to heart,

There is no place like home

In your arms.

Lips

Can I put my lips all over you?
And do the things that lovers do.
Can I kiss you up and down your back?
And slowly taste every inch of you.
Can I make love to you like never before?
You're in my heart like you wouldn't believe.
You're on my mind constantly.
All I can think of is
more More MORE.
More of you,
More of me.
More of us like it should be.
So can I put my lips all over you?
And make every day seem brand new.
With the love I have inside of me.
I guarantee your happiness,
I guarantee a morning kiss,
I guarantee just you and me.
If you'll just accept all of me.
My flaws, imperfections, and my voluptuous body.

Shantell Parson

But there are no flaws in my love for you.

Just take a chance on me.

So come to me and let us be.

Let us fulfill our destiny.

Let our hearts, our minds, and our bodies be one.

So let me put my lips all over you,

and prove day and night how much I love you.

All Night Long

Cum

Cum

Cum to me.

Let me rock the world you seek.

I can blow your mind day or night.

I can freak your body just right.

Slow or fast,

It doesn't matter.

'Cause what's between my legs,

is guaranteed to make you feel better.

Remember the feel when you first slid inside of me?

Good 'til the last drop,

Like Maxwell House coffee.

Your hard shaft driving in and out of me;

Coaxing every drop of cum outta me.

Afterwards we lay

side by side

as we hold each other tight.

Enjoying the aftershocks

rippling through my body.

Shantell Parson
No! No!
Please don't stop!
Practice makes perfect,
Lets wear our bodies out!